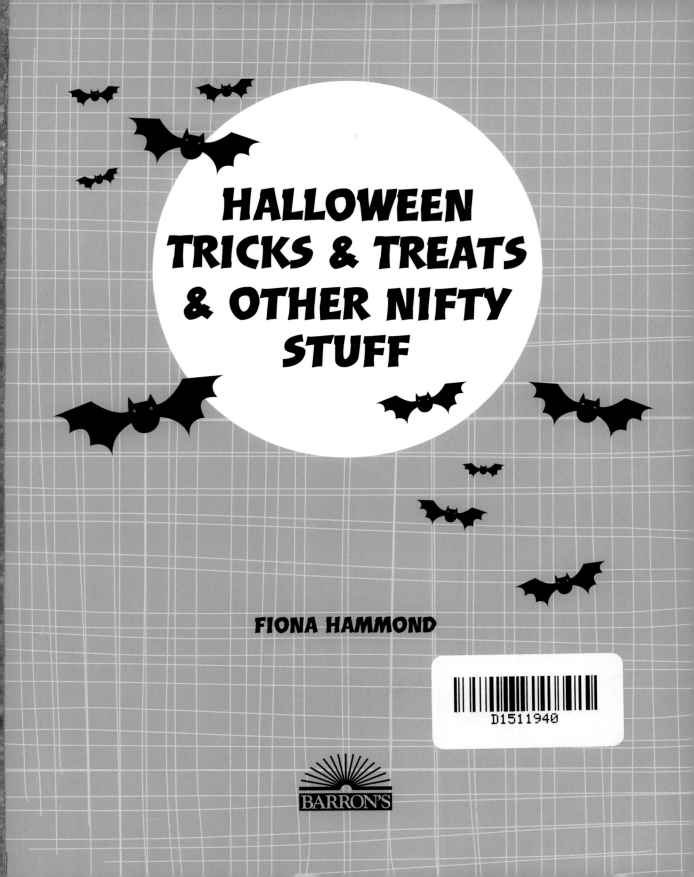

HALLOWEEN TRICKS & TREATS & OTHER NIFTY STUFF

FIONA HAMMOND

BARRON'S

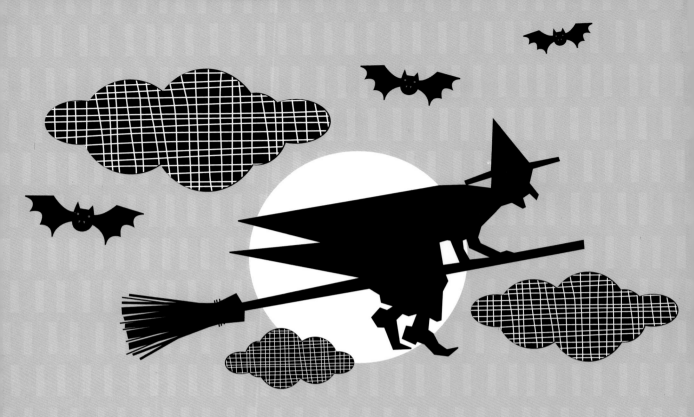

First edition for the United States and Canada published
in 2012 by Barron's Educational Series, Inc.

Copyright © 2011 by Five Mile Press Pty Ltd
1 Centre Road, Scoresby
Victoria 3179 Australia

All inquiries should be addressed to:
Barron's Educational Series, Inc.
250 Wireless Boulevard
Hauppauge, NY 11788
www.barronseduc.com

ISBN: 978-1-4380-0175-3

Library of Congress Control Number: 2012930212

Recipes and styling: Fiona Hammond
Design and illustration: Natalie Marshall
Photography: Greg Elms Photography

Product conforms to all applicable CPSC and CPSIA 2008
standards. No lead or phthalate hazard.

Warning!: This book contains recipes. Adult supervision
is advised when children prepare these recipes.

Printed in China
9 8 7 6 5 4 3 2

CONTENTS

WHITE-AS-A-GHOST MERINGUES

MAKES 40 GHOSTS

INGREDIENTS

1 quantity of meringue
(page 10)

2 tablespoons icing
(confectioners') sugar

1/2 teaspoon water

1 licorice stick with
colored center

EQUIPMENT

2 baking trays

baking paper

small bowl

metal spoon

small knife

piping bag fitted with plain
2/5 in. (1 cm) nozzle

BEFORE YOU START

Line 2 baking trays with baking
paper. Preheat the oven to 300° F
(150° C).

1. Spoon the meringue into the
piping bag.

2. Pipe fat and blobby lines
in rough "S" shapes onto the
prepared trays. Try to taper the
lines at the top and bottom—to
do this, you start by squeezing
the piping bag very gently, then
squeeze faster in the middle of
the line, then squeeze gently
again at the end. Your lines
should look roughly like ghosts!
Leave a little space between the
ghosts to allow for spreading.

3. Place the trays in the oven
and reduce the temperature to
210° F (100° C). Bake the ghosts
for 1 hour, then turn the oven

off and leave the door slightly
open for the meringues to cool
completely.

4. Put the icing sugar and water
in a small bowl and stir to form
a paste.

5. Cut the licorice stick into very
thin slices, which will be eyes for
the ghosts.

6. Dab a little icing onto the
back of the licorice slices and
stick them onto the ghosts for
eyes. Store the cooled ghosts
in an airtight container for up
to 1 week.

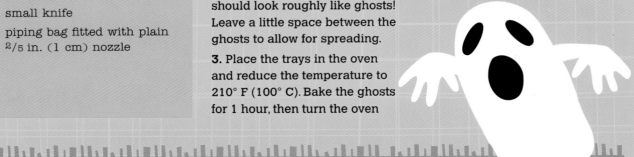

SPOOKY GHOSTLY CAPTIVES

CREATE
A SPOOKY
ATMOSPHERE
AT HALLOWEEN
WITH THESE
GHOSTLY LITTLE
CAPTIVES.

YOU WILL NEED

- ghost stencil
- pencil
- baking paper
- scissors
- medium- to large-sized jars to
  fit varying heights of ghosts
- Blu-Tack
- silver glitter

1. Trace the ghost stencil onto
baking paper. You can modify the
size of your ghost by enlarging or

reducing it depending on the
size of your jar.

2. Cut out your ghost. You could
also cut out eyes and mouth for
the ghost.

3. Attach the ghost's hands to
the side of the jar with Blu-Tack.

4. Fill the bottom of your jar with
silver glitter for an eerie touch.

HOT TIP!

Label your ghostly captive and
give it a name, such as "Fiery
Phantom" or "Grisly Ghoul."

BLIND MICE WITH LICORICE TAILS

MAKES 12 MICE

INGREDIENTS

4 oz (120 g) ginger-nut cookies

4 tablespoons smooth peanut butter

1 tablespoon unsalted butter, softened

$^1/_3$ cup (1$^1/_2$ oz/40 g) icing (confectioners') sugar

2 ft 6 in. (75 cm) licorice lace, cut into 12 lengths of 2$^1/_2$ in. (6 cm)

24 large sugar-coated chocolates such as M&Ms

EQUIPMENT

food processor

mixing bowl

small bowl

wooden spoon

skewer

small knife

1. Break the cookies into a food processor and blend to fine crumbs. Divide the crumbs between a mixing bowl and a smaller bowl, putting an even amount into each one.

2. Add the peanut butter, butter, and icing sugar to the mixing bowl of crumbs and stir until well combined.

3. Break the mixture into 12 even pieces and roll into balls. Shape each ball into a mouse by gently squeezing the dough between your thumb and first finger to form a pointy nose at one end of the ball.

4. Toss each mouse in the remaining bowl of cookie crumbs, coating all over. Place the mice on a tray and chill in the refrigerator for 10 minutes to firm up.

5. Use a skewer to poke a hole in the tail end of each mouse, going about $^2/_5$ in. (1 cm) deep. Push a length of licorice into the hole to form a tail.

6. Use the tip of a small knife to cut 2 slits on either side of each mouse's head. Press 2 sugar-coated chocolates of the same color into the slits to form ears.

You can store the mice in an airtight container in the refrigerator for up to 1 week.

RIP COFFIN TREATS BOX

THESE BONE-FILLED COFFINS ARE THE PERFECT PARTY TREATS TO HAND OUT TO YOUR FEARSOME FRIENDS.

YOU WILL NEED:

• coffin template from page 44, enlarged to 150%

• sheets of dark gray cardboard

• pencil

• scissors

• black marker pen

• glue stick

• white chalk

1. Make as many copies as you need of the coffin box template onto dark gray cardboard.

2. Use a black marker pen to write RIP onto the front of the box. (You might like to write the name of your guest underneath it for added effect!)

3. Fold the shape into a box using glue to secure the bottom and side.

4. Rub the edges of the coffin box with white chalk to give it a weathered effect.

5. Fill the box with some small treats.

HOT TIP!

For a simple trick-or-treat bag to fill with goodies, why not decorate small brown paper bags using the stickers and other shapes from the templates on page 48 and the stencil sheet at the back of this book.

PUMPKIN FACE DECORATIONS

YOU WILL NEED:

• orange paper or plastic plate

• pumpkin stalk and pumpkin mouth, nose, and eyes templates from page 48

• tracing paper or baking paper

• pencil

• sheet of green cardboard

• scissors

• glue stick

• black cardboard

• Blu-Tack

1. Trace the pumpkin stalk, mouth, nose, and eyes templates.

2. Transfer the stalk template onto green cardboard and cut it out. Use glue to affix the stalk to the top of the pumpkin.

3. Transfer the pumpkin mouth, nose, and eyes onto black cardboard. Use glue to affix them onto the orange plate.

4. Attach your pumpkin face with Blu-Tack to your front door to greet trick-or-treaters.

MAKE SOME SCARY PUMPKIN FACE DECORATIONS TO HANG ON YOUR FRONT DOOR FOR TRICK-OR-TREATERS.

MERINGUE BONES

**MAKES 60 SMALL OR
40 LARGE BONES**

INGREDIENTS

3 egg whites

pinch of cream of tartar

3/4 cup (5 1/2 oz/165 g)
caster (superfine) sugar

EQUIPMENT

2 baking trays

baking paper

mixing bowl

electric beaters

metal spoon

piping bag fitted with
plain 2/5 in. (1 cm) nozzle

BEFORE YOU START

Line 2 baking trays with baking
paper. Preheat the oven to 300° F
(150° C).

1. Put the egg whites and cream
of tartar in a clean, dry mixing
bowl and beat with electric
beaters until soft peaks begin
to form.

2. Continue to beat the egg
whites while you add the sugar
a spoonful at a time. Beat until
the mixture is glossy and thick,
and the peaks hold up firmly
when the beaters are lifted out.

3. Spoon the meringue into the
piping bag. Pipe the meringue
in bone shapes (sticks with
knobbly ends) onto the prepared
trays. You might like to do some
small bones about 2 in. (5 cm)
long, and some longer bones
about 4 in. (10 cm) long. Leave
a little space between the bones
to allow for spreading.

4. Place the trays in the oven
and reduce the temperature to
210° F (100° C). Bake the bones

for 1 hour, then turn the oven
off and leave the door slightly
open for the meringues to cool
completely. (You can place the
handle of a wooden spoon in the
door opening.)

5. Store the cooled bones in
an airtight container for up to
1 week.

HOT TIPS!

**To separate eggs, get 2 bowls
ready. Crack an egg, then hold
it in one hand and gently open
it with your thumb. Tip the
egg into the cupped palm of
your other hand, holding your
hand above a bowl. Open your
fingers slightly and allow the
white to slip through into the
bowl, then drop the yolk into
the other bowl.**

Decoration Tip

You can serve these bones in
a jar with a fun label attached.
Or you can put them inside the
coffin boxes (see page 9) and
give them away as a Halloween
treat.

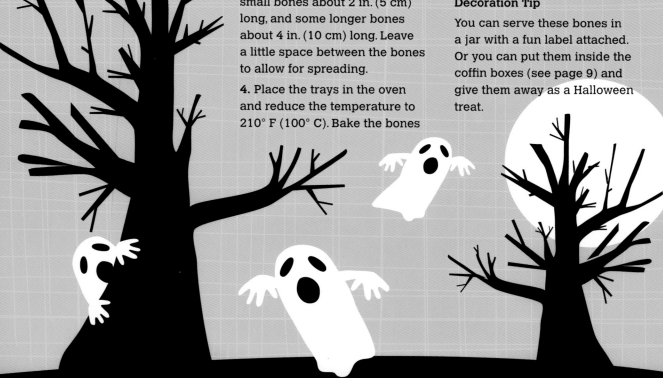

CHOCOLATE TOMBSTONE CAKES

MAKES 16 CAKES

CAKES

1 1/2 cups (8 oz/225 g)
self-raising flour

1/2 cup (2 oz/60 g) cocoa

1 1/2 teaspoons bicarbonate
of soda

1 1/4 cups (10 oz/275 g)
caster (superfine) sugar

6 oz (180 g) unsalted butter

7 fl oz (200 ml) buttermilk

1 teaspoon vanilla extract

3 eggs

CHOCOLATE ICING

10 1/2 oz (300 g) dark
chocolate, broken into pieces

2 oz (60 g) unsalted butter

3 tablespoons golden syrup

WHITE ICING

1 cup (4 oz/120 g) icing
(confectioners') sugar

2–3 teaspoons water

GRASS

2 cups (1 lb/440 g)
white sugar

1 teaspoon green
food coloring

EQUIPMENT

2 mini rectangular cake
trays (holes measuring
3 1/2 x 2 in./8.5 x 5 cm),
to make 16 cakes

baking paper, sieve,
mixing bowls, saucepans,
metal spoon, electric beaters,
skewer, wire rack,
chopping board,
small serrated knife,
small spatula, small whisk,
plastic zip-lock bag,
scissors, large platter

BEFORE YOU START

Butter 16 mini rectangular
cake holes and line the bases
with rectangles of baking
paper. Preheat the oven
to 345° F (175° C).

1. Sift the flour, cocoa,
bicarbonate of soda, and sugar
into a large mixing bowl. Make
a well in the center.

2. Put the butter in a medium
saucepan and place over low
heat. Stir until it melts, then
remove from the heat. Stir in the
buttermilk, vanilla, and eggs.

3. Pour the butter mixture into
the well of dry ingredients.
Use electric beaters to beat the
mixture together for 5 minutes.

4. Divide the mixture between
the cake holes. Bake the cakes in
the oven for 20 minutes, or until
a skewer comes out clean when
inserted in the middle of the cake.
Cool the cakes in the tins for
10 minutes, then remove and
place on a wire rack and leave
to cool completely.

5. To make the chocolate icing,
place the chocolate in a small
heatproof bowl. Set the bowl
over a small saucepan of gently
simmering water, making sure
the bowl doesn't touch the water.
Stir until the chocolate melts,
then remove from the heat.

6. Stir the butter and golden
syrup into the melted chocolate
until well combined. Set the
mixture aside to cool for
10 minutes.

7. Take 1 cake and place it
upside down on a chopping
board. Use a serrated knife to
trim one end of the cake into an
arch like the top of a tombstone.
Trim the other end to a flat
base so the cake can stand up.
Continue trimming the remaining
cakes and place onto wire rack.
Reserve all the cake off-cuts.

8. Use a spatula to spread the
chocolate icing smoothly over
the cake bottoms and around
the sides, leaving the cut base
free for the cakes to stand up on
the wire rack. Then put in the
refrigerator for 10–15 minutes,
until the chocolate icing sets.

9. To make the white icing, sift
the icing sugar into a bowl. Use
a whisk to mix in enough water
to make a smooth, thick paste.

10. Transfer the icing to a
zip-lock bag and seal. Use
scissors to snip a very small hole
in a corner of the bag. Gently
squeeze the icing toward the
hole and slowly pipe decorations
onto the cakes, such as outlines
around the tombstones and
crucifixes. Set the decorated
cakes aside for 10 minutes to
allow the white icing to set.

11. To make the "grass," put the
sugar in a mixing bowl and stir
in the green food coloring until
the sugar is evenly colored.
Spread over a large platter.

12. Stand the tombstones on
the grass. Crumble the cake
off-cuts and mound in front
of the tombstones to represent
the soil of the graves.

BRILLIANT BROOMSTICKS

YOU WILL NEED

• 3 large brown paper bags

• twine or rope

• scissors

• a sturdy stick (long and thick enough to be a broom handle for a young child)

• sticky tape

HOT TIP!

If you cannot find a stick long enough for a broomstick, use a piece of dowel or an old broom.

1. To make the fringe for the broom, lay one large brown paper bag flat on the table with the folded end toward you.

2. Start from the folded part of the bag, make cuts roughly 1 1/4 in. (3 cm) apart (creating the bristles of the broom). Stop 4 in. (10 cm) before the open end. Repeat with the second paper bag.

3. Put one end of the stick into the mouth of the remaining paper bag and cinch it around the stick. Tape to secure.

4. Secure the other two paper bag fringes to the stick with sticky tape.

5. Wind twine or rope around the broomstick where the paper bags are attached to hold them in place and to add that special touch.

6. For an extra treat, add some lollipops in the whole paper bag before securing it to the stick. It can be given away as a prize!

CHOCOLATE LICORICE BROOMSTICKS

MAKES 8 BROOMSTICKS

INGREDIENTS

7 yards (6.5 meters) licorice lace

8 licorice sticks

10 1/2 oz (300 g) dark chocolate, broken into pieces

EQUIPMENT

tray

baking paper

scissors

small heatproof bowl

small saucepan

metal spoon

1. Line a tray with baking paper.

2. Use scissors to cut the licorice lace into 8 long lengths of 8 in. (20 cm) and 80 short lengths of 2½ in. (6 cm).

3. Gather 10 short lengths and hold them in a bundle—this is the "straw" of the broomstick. Insert a licorice stick inside the bundle, going about 1 1/4 in. (3 cm) down like a handle.

4. Wrap a long length of licorice tightly around the top of the bundle to secure it to the handle (the licorice should be sticky enough that you won't need to tie a knot). Continue making broomsticks with the remaining licorice lace and sticks.

5. Place the chocolate in a small heatproof bowl. Set the bowl over a small saucepan of gently simmering water, making sure the bowl doesn't touch the water. Stir until the chocolate melts, then remove from the heat.

6. Take a broomstick and dip the straw end into the melted chocolate, swirling it around to coat the licorice strands all over. Remove from the chocolate and allow any excess to drip back into the bowl. Lay on the prepared tray and continue to dip the remaining broomsticks. Place the tray of broomsticks in the refrigerator for 30 minutes to set the chocolate.

7. The broomsticks can be stored in an airtight container in a cool place for up to 1 week.

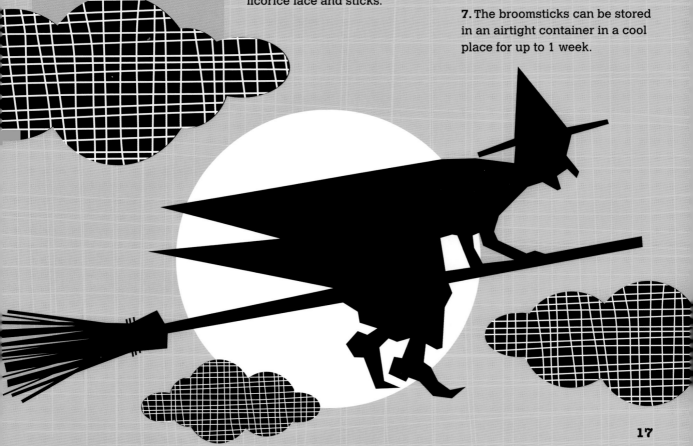

CHOCOLATE BAT COOKIES

MAKES 15 COOKIES

INGREDIENTS

4 oz (125 g) unsalted butter, softened

2/3 cup (4 oz/120 g) brown sugar

1 egg

2 tablespoons golden syrup

2 3/4 cups (14 1/2 oz/410 g) plain (all-purpose) flour

1/4 cup (1 oz/30 g) cocoa

1 teaspoon baking powder

EQUIPMENT

2 baking trays

mixing bowl

electric beaters

sieve

bat stencil from back of book

wooden spoon

plastic wrap

rolling pin

small knife

small funnel

wire rack

1. Line 2 baking trays with baking paper.

2. Put the butter and sugar in a mixing bowl and beat with electric beaters until pale and creamy. Add the egg and beat well. Add the golden syrup and beat until just combined.

3. Sift the flour, cocoa, and baking powder onto the butter mixture. Use a wooden spoon to stir the mixture together until it forms a dough. Use your hands to shape the dough into a disc, then cover it with plastic wrap and refrigerate for 30 minutes.

4. Preheat the oven to 345° F (175° C). Tear off 2 large pieces of baking paper and place one on your work surface. Unwrap the chilled dough and put it in the middle of the paper, then cover with the other sheet of paper. Use a rolling pin to roll the dough out inside the paper to a large piece 1/5 in. (5 mm) thick. If it is sticking to the paper, you can sprinkle it lightly with flour.

5. Lay your bat stencil over the dough and cut out a bat by going around the stencil with the tip of a small knife. Transfer the bat to a prepared baking tray, then continue to cut out as many more bats as you can fit across the dough.

6. Cut out 2 eyes in each bat by pressing the narrow end of a small funnel into the bat's face, then removing the small circles of dough.

7. Collect all the pastry scraps, form them into a ball, and roll out again between the sheets of baking paper. Cut out more bats.

8. Bake the bats in the oven for 10 minutes. Leave to cool on the trays for 5 minutes, then transfer to a wire rack to cool completely.

Hot Tip!

Whenever dough becomes too soft to work with, place it in the refrigerator for 10 minutes to firm it up.

CREEPY CHOCOLATE SPIDERS

MAKES 12 SPIDERS

INGREDIENTS

2 oz (50 g) dried fried Asian noodles

3 oz (90 g) dark chocolate, broken into pieces

mini sugar-coated chocolates such as M&Ms

EQUIPMENT

tray

baking paper

heatproof mixing bowl

saucepan

metal spoon

1. Line a tray with baking paper.

2. The noodles need to be in roughly 1¹⁄₄ in. (3 cm) lengths. If yours are longer, put them in a bowl and gently crush them with your hands until the right length.

3. Place the chocolate in a heatproof mixing bowl. Set the bowl over a saucepan of gently simmering water, making sure the bowl doesn't touch the water. Stir until the chocolate melts, then remove from the heat and allow to cool for 5 minutes.

4. Stir the noodles into the melted chocolate until the noodles are thoroughly coated.

5. Mound tablespoons of the chocolate-coated noodles onto the prepared tray. Adjust the mounds by pulling out noodle "legs" so the mounds look like spiders.

6. Stick 2 sugar-coated chocolates of the same color onto each spider for eyes.

7. Put the tray of spiders in the refrigerator for 15 minutes, or until the chocolate has set. Transfer to an airtight container and store in the refrigerator for up to 5 days.

BERRY BLOOD SLUSH WITH GLOWING HAND

SERVES 8

INGREDIENTS

orange juice to fill glove
(around 10 fl oz/300 ml),
plus 4 fl oz (125 ml)
for slush

1 lb 5 oz (600 g) frozen
raspberries

1/3 cup (1 1/2 oz/40 g)
icing (confectioners') sugar

EQUIPMENT

disposable glove

food processor

large serving bowl

scissors

serving glasses

metal spoon

serving spoons

1. Rinse the glove under running water to remove any powder coating, then shake all the water out. Get someone to help you to hold the glove open while you pour orange juice in, leaving room at the top to tie a knot.

Tie the knot, sealing the orange juice inside the glove. Freeze for at least 4 hours (overnight is best, as you want the juice to be completely frozen).

2. Put the berries, icing sugar, and 4 fl oz (125 ml) of orange juice in a food processor and blend until smooth. Pour into a large serving bowl.

3. Use scissors to carefully cut and peel the glove off the frozen orange-juice hand. Place the hand on top of the berry slush.

4. Serve quickly before the slush begins to melt. Spoon the slush into glasses, then break off parts of the orange-juice hand and place on top. Serve with spoons.

SHUDDERSOME SPIDERS

DO SPIDERS GIVE YOU THE HEEBIE-JEEBIES? SCARE YOUR GUESTS WITH A CLUSTER OF ALARMING ARACHNIDS!

YOU WILL NEED

• large egg carton

• black paint

• scissors or wooden skewer

• 16 black pipe cleaners,
3 3/4 in. (8 cm) in length

• 8 googly eyes, 1/4 in. (6 mm)
in diameter

• craft glue

1. Paint your egg carton black.

2. For the body of the spider, cut out an egg cup from the carton.

3. Hold the body hollow-side down and, with the pointy end of the scissors or a wooden skewer, make four holes on each side.

4. Insert a pipe cleaner into each hole and thread through to the other side for legs. Bend them slightly at the end to create feet.

5. Stick two googly eyes onto the face of the spider.

DREADFUL DOORKNOB HANGERS

DANGLE THIS DREADFUL DOOR HANGER FROM YOUR DOORKNOB TO FOREWARN YOUR GUESTS ABOUT WHAT AWAITS INSIDE!

YOU WILL NEED:

- doorknob hanger template from page 45
- tracing paper or baking paper
- colored cardboard of your choice
- scissors
- glue stick
- colored pens and lead pencil
- foil stickers for decorating

1. Trace the doorknob hanger template onto a sheet of colored cardboard.

2. Use the shapes from the templates on page 48 and the stencil sheet to decorate your doorknob hanger.

3. Add a shiny touch to your decoration with some of the stickers in this book.

4. Create a message on your doorknob hanger to greet your guests on Halloween. Some examples are:

QUIET! YOU MAY WAKE THE DEAD

ENTER... GHOSTS ABIDE HERE!

BEWARE OF A SCARE!

JOIN THE MAYHEM

TRICK OR TREAT!

SHIFTY FRANKENSTEIN SHADOW

GIVE YOUR FAMILY A SCARE WITH SOME CREATIVE SHADOW THEATRE. FUN FOR YOUNG AND OLD !

YOU WILL NEED:

- large black cardboard
- tracing paper
- pencil
- Frankenstein parts templates from pages 46 and 47
- package of brass fasteners
- hole punch
- wooden skewer, approximately 12 in. (30 cm) in length

1. Make copies of the body parts of Frankenstein and cut them out.

2. Trace each body part onto black cardboard, taking care to mark out where the holes need to be punched.

3. Use a hole puncher to make holes where indicated, and attach arms and legs to the torso using the brass fasteners. The brass fasteners will allow you to move the limbs so that you can put your Frankenstein into different poses.

4. Tape the wooden skewer to the Frankenstein's body.

5. Set up a lamp pointed at a blank wall and create shifty shadows with your new bolt-headed friend.

HOT TIP!

Cutting out the eyes and mouth can be tricky so ask a grown-up for help.

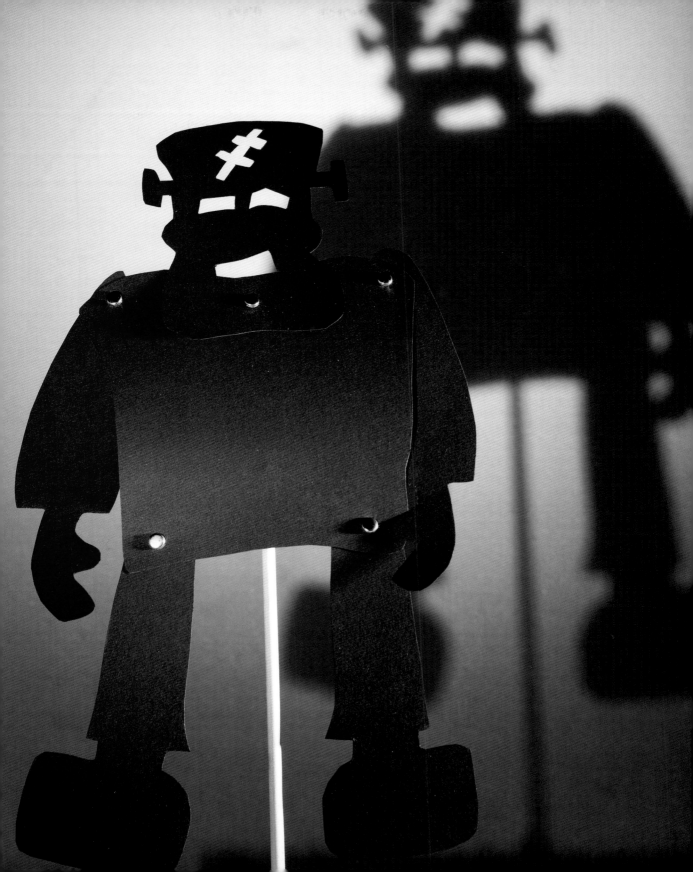

FRANKENSTEIN FIZZ

SERVES 6

INGREDIENTS

$^1/_2$ cup (2 oz/60 g) icing (confectioners') sugar

$1^1/_2$ tablespoons citric acid

3 teaspoons bicarbonate of soda

6 licorice sticks

EQUIPMENT

6 small bottles with lids (necks wide enough to fit licorice in)

sieve

mixing bowl

whisk

metal spoon

funnel

labels

jar for the licorice

BEFORE YOU START

Wash your 6 bottles and lids and allow them to dry thoroughly.

1. Sift the icing sugar, citric acid, and bicarbonate of soda into a mixing bowl. Whisk to combine.

2. Spoon the mixture into your bottles through a funnel. Seal the bottles with the lids.

3. Decorate the bottles with your own labels.

4. Serve the bottles with a jar of licorice sticks alongside. Then take a licorice stick, dip it into your fizz, and suck for a fizzy, tingling sensation.

HOT TIP!

Make sure you seal your bottles well, as otherwise the fizz will absorb moisture from the air.

LEGGY SPIDER LOLLIPOPS

MAKE SOME CHARMING SPIDERS TO GIVE AWAY AS TREATS TO YOUR FRIENDS! MAKES SIX POPS.

YOU WILL NEED

• Six $4^1/_2$ in. (12 cm) square black or dark red cellophane sheets

• ruler

• scissors

• 6 lollipops

• 24 black pipe cleaners, 12 in. (30 cm) in length

• 12 googly eyes, $^1/_4$ in. (6 mm) in diameter

• craft glue

1. Place the center of the cellophane over the top of the lollipop and pull tight around the stick.

2. Wrap the center of one pipe cleaner around the stick at the base of the lollipop, making sure that the legs end up the same length.

3. Wrap the other three pipe cleaners in the same way. You should have eight legs.

4. Glue the googly eyes onto the head of the spider. Repeat steps for the other crafty critters.

BLOOD-SHOT EYEBALL COOKIES

MAKES 24 COOKIES

INGREDIENTS

4 oz (125 g) unsalted butter, softened

3/4 cup (5 1/2 oz/165 g) caster (superfine) sugar

2 eggs

2 cups (10 1/2 oz/300 g) plain (all-purpose) flour

1 teaspoon baking powder

3 tablespoons raspberry jam

12 rounded sugar-dusted jujubes

24 mini sugar-coated chocolates such as M&Ms

red food coloring

EQUIPMENT

2 baking trays

baking paper

mixing bowl

electric beaters

sieve

wooden spoon

teaspoon

small knife

fine paintbrush

BEFORE YOU START

Preheat the oven to 350° F (180° C). Line 2 baking trays with baking paper.

1. Put the butter and sugar in a mixing bowl and beat with electric beaters until pale and creamy. Add the eggs one at a time, beating well after each addition.

2. Sift the flour and baking powder onto the butter mixture. Use a wooden spoon to stir the mixture together until it forms a soft dough.

3. Break off walnut-sized pieces of dough and roll them into balls. Place on the prepared baking trays. Gently press down on each ball to flatten it slightly.

4. Make a shallow hole in the center of each cookie using the end of the wooden spoon (make sure you don't poke all the way through). Spoon 1/2 teaspoon of jam into each hole.

5. Cut the jujubes in half horizontally using a small knife. Place half a jujube cut-side up on top of the jam on each cookie, pushing the jujube down so a little jam oozes out the sides.

6. Bake the cookies in the oven for 10–15 minutes, until light golden. Place a mini sugar-coated chocolate in the center of each jujube and leave the cookies to cool on the trays (the chocolates will stick to the jujubes as the cookies cool).

7. Dip a fine paintbrush into red food coloring and paint thin branching lines around the edge of each cookie running toward the eyeball to resemble veins.

8. You can store the cookies in an airtight container for up to 1 week.

1 SCREAM AT BUGS

MAKES 6 ICE CREAMS

INGREDIENTS

vanilla ice cream
(or any other flavor)

6 ice-cream cones with
flat bases

9 oz (250 g) milk or dark
chocolate, broken into pieces

candies to decorate, such
as mini and regular-sized
sugar-coated chocolates
(i.e., M&Ms), sour worms,
jelly beans, and anything
else your imagination
desires!

EQUIPMENT

ice-cream scoop

tray

small heatproof bowl

small saucepan

metal spoon

1. Scoop a large, neat ball of
ice cream into the top of each
cone and press it down gently.
Stand the cones upright on a
tray and place in the freezer
for 10–15 minutes to set the
ice cream firmly in place.

2. Place the chocolate in a small
heatproof bowl. Set the bowl
over a small saucepan of gently
simmering water, making sure
the bowl doesn't touch the water.
Stir until the chocolate melts,
then remove from the heat.

3. Remove an ice cream from
the freezer. Hold it in one hand
and use your other hand to
slightly tilt the bowl of melted
chocolate. Dip the ice cream into
the chocolate and gently turn
it around until it is coated with
chocolate all over. Allow any
excess chocolate to drip back
into the bowl.

4. Stand the ice-cream cone on
a work surface and decorate the
top with candies, gently sticking
them into the wet chocolate. Use
your imagination to make the ice
cream look like a bug or monster,
such as by sticking on 2 large
sugar-coated chocolates for
eyes, 2 sour worms for antennas,
and lots of mini sugar-coated
chocolates over the monster's
belly. Return the decorated
ice cream to the freezer and
continue dipping and decorating
the remaining ice creams.

5. Leave the decorated ice
creams in the freezer for up to
2 hours before serving. (To store
them for longer, you can transfer
them to an airtight container or
individual cellophane bags once
the chocolate has set.)

WORM-INFESTED APPLES DIPPED IN BUBBLING MUD

MAKES 6 CARAMEL-COATED APPLES

INGREDIENTS

6 small nonwaxed organic apples

1 cup (8 oz/220 g) caster (superfine) sugar

3 tablespoons liquid glucose

2 tablespoons water

6$\frac{1}{2}$ fl oz (180 ml) cream

3$\frac{1}{2}$ oz (100 g) unsalted butter

12–18 sour-worm candies

EQUIPMENT

6 wooden toffee-apple sticks (available at catering suppliers), or six 8 in. (20 cm) lengths of a sturdy branch from an apple tree (or other fruit tree)

small bowl

ice

tray

baking paper

medium saucepan

metal spoon

sugar thermometer, if available

1. Wash the apples and dry them well. Remove any stalks. Push a stick into the center of each apple going from the top almost all the way to the bottom.

2. Prepare a small bowl of iced water (with about 6 ice cubes) and a tray lined with baking paper.

3. Put the sugar, glucose, and water in a medium saucepan and place over low heat. Stir until the sugar dissolves, then stop stirring, as otherwise the mixture can become lumpy and crystallize.

4. Add the butter and cream to the saucepan without stirring and increase the heat to medium. Bring the mixture to a boil and cook for 15–20 minutes, until the caramel reaches "soft-ball stage," which is when you can drop a small amount into the bowl of iced water and it forms a ball that you can shape in your fingers. Test the caramel regularly toward the end of the cooking time. (If you have a sugar thermometer, soft-ball stage is at 240° F (115° C).) Once you reach this stage, immediately remove the saucepan from the heat.

5. Working quickly while the caramel is hot, hold the stick of an apple in one hand and use your other hand to carefully tilt the saucepan of caramel. Twirl the apple in the caramel until evenly coated. Allow the excess caramel to drip back into the pan, then stand the apple on the prepared tray. Repeat with the remaining apples.

6. Dip the ends of your sour worms in the leftover caramel and stick them in place on the apples while the caramel is still warm.

7. Transfer the decorated apples to the refrigerator for 20 minutes for the caramel to set. (The caramel should set to a chewy consistency.) The apples will keep for up to 3 days in the refrigerator wrapped in baking paper or cellophane.

COME TO A
HALLOWEEN
PARTY!

YOU ARE
INVITED TO A
SCARE-AND-FRIGHT
NIGHT!

BATTY INVITATIONS

LOOKING FOR A FUN INVITE WITHOUT ANY FUSS? YOU CAN'T GO PAST THESE JIGGLING, BATTY SENSATIONS!

YOU WILL NEED:

- bat template from page 48 (or the witch or pumpkin templates)
- tracing paper or baking paper
- pencil
- scissors
- silver cardboard
- 2 black paper strips, $3/4$ in. x 6 in. (2 cm x 15 cm)
- 6 in. x 8 $1/4$ in. (15 cm x 21 cm) piece black cardboard
- glue stick
- silver pen
- glitter glue

1. Trace the bat template onto silver cardboard and cut it out.

2. Fold the two strips of black paper into accordion-style springs and glue the end of each strip onto the back of the bat.

3. Glue the other end of the springs to the bottom of the black cardboard.

4. Write details of your party onto the card with silver or black pen. Decorate your card using the foil stickers in the book.

5. Slide the card into an envelope.

6. When your guest pulls the invite from the envelope, the bat will pop out at them!

WITCHES ON BROOMSTICKS

YOU WILL NEED:

- witch stencil
- pencil
- sheet of black cardboard (one sheet is enough for 2 witches)
- scissors
- sticky tape
- long pencils or wooden skewers

1. Trace the witch stencil onto a sheet of black cardboard.

2. Cut out the witch shape, taking extra care around the face and hair.

3. Secure the witch onto the side of a long pencil or wooden skewers, using sticky tape.

4. For the broom head, cut out a black triangle and fringe one side to stick to the end of the pencil.

5. Use your witches on brooms as wooden skewers for party nibbles such as cheese or pickled onions, or give away the witches on broom pencils as treats.

HOT TIP!

Use the templates or stencil shapes from this book to decorate your pens and pencils with other creatures or ghouls!

IN THE MOOD FOR SOME SPOOKY STATIONERY? TREAT YOUR GHOULISH GANG WITH THESE WICKED WITCH FAVORITES.

SPIDERWEB PUMPKIN SOUP

SERVES 4–6

INGREDIENTS

2 tablespoons olive oil

1 onion, finely chopped

2 lb 10 oz (1.3 kg) pumpkin, peeled, seeded, and thinly sliced

1 1/2 teaspoons garam marsala

1 teaspoon ground cumin

17 fl oz (500 ml) chicken stock

17 fl oz (500 ml) water

sea salt

4 fl oz (125 ml) cream

EQUIPMENT

knife

chopping board

large saucepan

wooden spoon

stick blender

plastic zip-lock bag

ladle

soup tureen

toothpick

1. Heat the oil in a large saucepan over medium heat. Add the onion and fry for 5 minutes, stirring every so often, until softened.

2. Stir in the pumpkin and spices and cook, stirring for another 2 minutes.

3. Add the stock and water and bring to a boil, then reduce the heat to low and simmer for 20 minutes, or until the pumpkin is tender. Remove from the heat.

4. Use a stick blender to blend the soup to a smooth puree. Season with salt to taste.

5. Pour the cream into a zip-lock bag and seal it shut.

6. Ladle the soup into a large tureen. Snip a very small hole in a corner of the zip-lock bag. Squeeze the cream toward the hole and slowly pipe a large spiral on the surface of the soup beginning from near the outside edge and going almost all the way to the center. Each circle of the spiral should be about 2/5 in. (1 cm) apart.

7. Dip the tip of a toothpick into the center of the soup and carefully drag it in a straight line toward the edge of the tureen or bowl, pulling out the circles of cream. Continue to drag lines around the soup, creating a spiderweb effect.

GREEN GLOOP (WITH BAT'S BLOOD) AND GHOULY TORTILLAS

SERVES 6

INGREDIENTS

6 soft tortillas, 8 in. (20 cm) in diameter

2 avocados

1 tablespoon lemon juice

1 tomato, diced

1/2 red onion, finely chopped

2 tablespoons chopped coriander leaves

sea salt

freshly ground black pepper

Tabasco sauce (or other chili sauce)

EQUIPMENT

scissors

small funnel

2 baking trays

knife

metal spoon

medium bowl

fork

serving bowl

1. Preheat the oven to 300° F (150° C).

2. Use scissors to cut each tortilla into 4 triangles or quarters. These triangles are your ghouly ghosts, but to make them spookier you can round off the corners and also trim the sides so the ghosts are a bit wobbly, not straight.

3. Use the narrow end of a small funnel to cut out eyes for the ghosts.

4. Spread the ghosts in one layer over the baking trays. Bake in the oven for 10 minutes, or until the ghosts are crisp and golden around the edges. Transfer to a wire rack to cool.

5. Cut the avocados in half, remove the stones, and use a spoon to scoop out the flesh, putting it into a medium bowl. Add the lemon juice and mash the avocado coarsely with a fork.

6. Add the tomato, onion, and coriander, and stir gently to combine. Season with salt and pepper.

7. Transfer the avocado dip (called guacamole) to a serving bowl and add a few drops of Tabasco sauce to the top to look like fresh bat's blood. Serve with the ghouly ghosts.

PIN THE NOSE ON THE JACK-O'-LANTERN

YOU WILL NEED:

• Jack-O'-Lantern poster from back of the book

• scissors

• Blu-Tack

1. Remove the Jack-O'-Lantern poster from the back of this book.

2. Cut along the dotted lines at the bottom of the poster to remove the strip of "noses."

3. Cut out the noses for the game.

4. Insert a thumbtack on each nose for each player.

5. Players take turn blindfolded and try to pin their noses in the right place on the pumpkin.

HERE'S A GAME TO KEEP YOUR HALLOWEEN PARTY GUESTS MOVING AND GIGGLING WITH GHOULISH DELIGHT!

It was the custom for many years at Halloween to carry hollowed-out turnips carved to look like faces. This is the origin of the modern Jack-o'-Lantern.

Irish people who came to live in America found that it was much easier to carve pumpkins than turnips, so the pumpkin lantern became the decoration which many people associate most with Halloween.

Pumpkin carving in recent years has become an art form. At Halloween not only fearsome faces have been carved into the pumpkins, but also all kinds of weird and awesome designs.

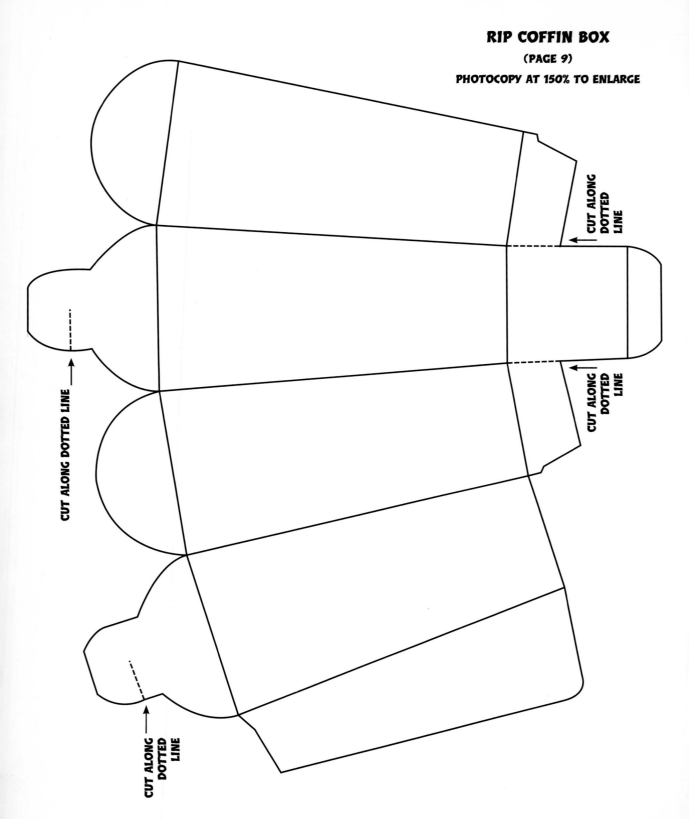

RIP COFFIN BOX
(PAGE 9)
PHOTOCOPY AT 150% TO ENLARGE

CUT ALONG DOTTED LINE

CUT ALONG DOTTED LINE

CUT ALONG DOTTED LINE

CUT ALONG DOTTED LINE

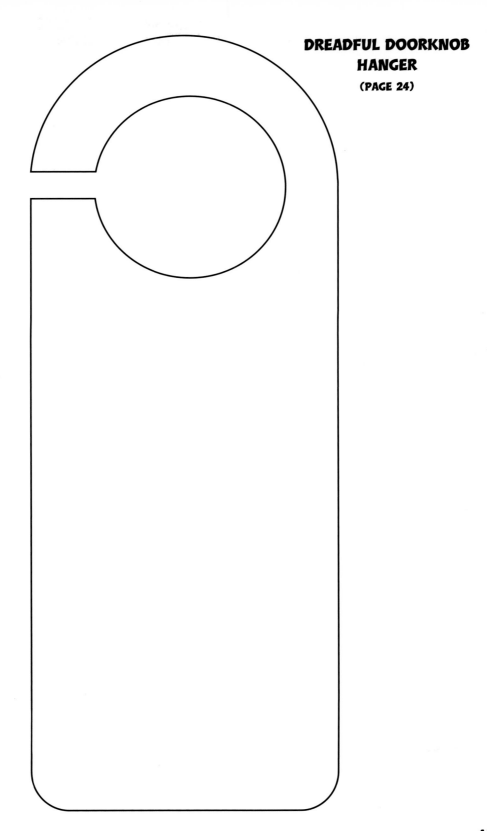

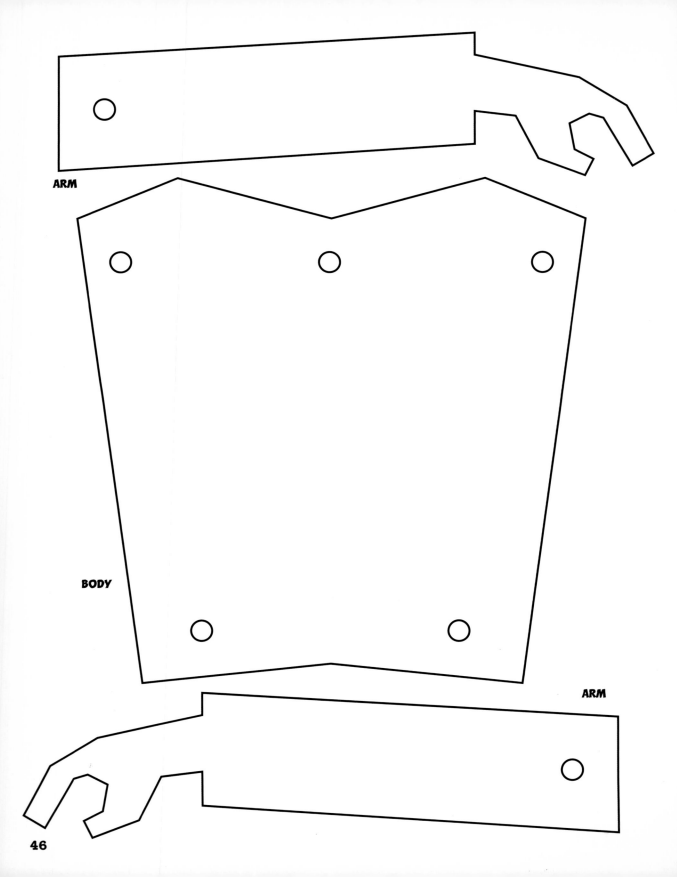

ARM

BODY

ARM

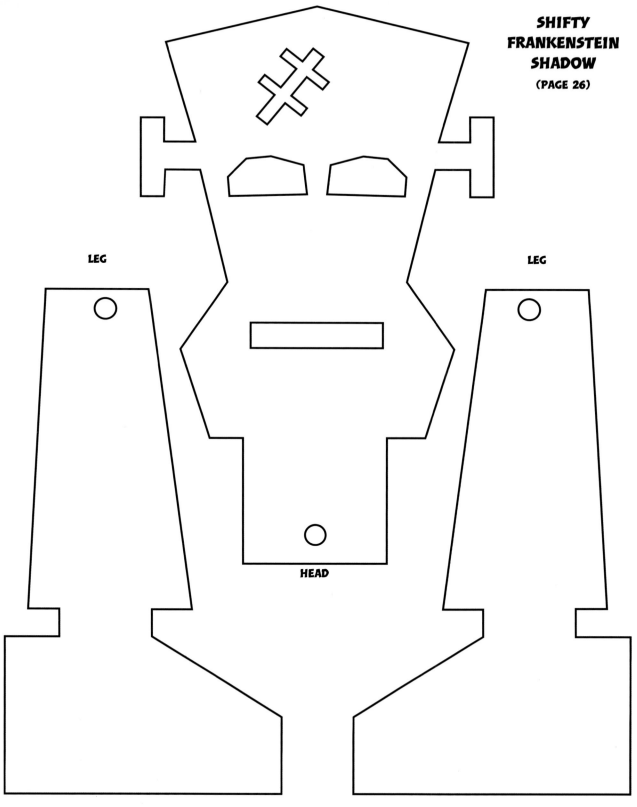

SHIFTY
FRANKENSTEIN
SHADOW

(PAGE 26)

LEG

LEG

HEAD

BAT, WITCH, AND PUMPKIN

(PAGES 9, 25, 37)

PUMPKIN FACE DECORATION

(PAGE 9)